11303

Norwood Grade School Library
Dist. R 2 Jt.

WITHDRAWN
www.loneconelibrary.org

Sports World

Judo

Donna Bailey

STECK-VAUGHN
L I B R A R Y
A Division of Steck-Vaughn Company

11303

I am going to learn judo.
We wear loose white pants and
special jackets with thick collars.
The belt is tied in a special way
so it won't come undone.

2

Judo belts come in different colors.
The belt color shows a person's rank.
My belt is white because I am
just beginning judo.
The highest rank is a black belt.

At the beginning of the class,
we kneel down and bow to our teacher.

We start our lesson by
rolling around on the mat.
Rolling around like this is fun.
It teaches us how to relax our body.

Next we learn how to curl up and
roll forward like a ball.

When I come out of a roll
I throw my arm out to the side.
My arm and hand must be flat
when they hit the mat.

Next we learn how to fall backward.
I remember to fall with
my arms and hands out.
This keeps me from getting hurt.

8

Now we practice in pairs.
We learn how to tumble over
each other and roll onto our side.

We bow to our partner before
the next activity.

10

Our teacher shows us how to
hold on to our partner.
I grip his collar with my right hand
and his right sleeve with my left hand.

My partner swings his hip against me.
He tries to throw me onto the ground.
I lose my balance and let my body relax.
I let myself go forward with the throw.

I do not hurt myself when I land
because I've learned how to fall.

Now it is my turn to try to
throw my partner.
After a while I can lift him off
the ground and throw him, too.

14

At the end of the lesson we have
a free practice, or randori.
I try to throw one of the bigger girls.

At first we struggle, but she knows
more judo than I do.
She turns me against her hip and
I lose my balance.

16

When I lose my balance, I let my body
move in the direction of the throw.
When I relax and fall the right way
I do not get hurt.

Judo students try to throw their partner.
In judo, skill is more important
than a person's size.
This boy is throwing a partner
much bigger than he is.

18

This woman has just thrown her partner,
using a standing throw.
Her partner flings out his arms
to break his fall.

Norwood Grade School Library
Dist. R 2 Jt.

This man threw his partner over
his right shoulder.
The man keeps hold of his partner's
right sleeve and straightens up
after the throw.

To become skilled in judo, you must learn
many different moves.
Sometimes you use your feet or
legs to unbalance your partner.

You also learn how to
hold down someone who
is struggling to escape.

It is difficult to get out of this hold!
You can use your legs as well as
your arms to pin someone to
the ground.

When you want to get out of a hold,
you tap your partner or the mat lightly.
This shows that you give in and
your partner has won.

24

In a judo match, you score points for
how long you can hold someone down
on the mat.

Judo matches and shows have made judo
a popular sport for people of all ages.

The color of your belt shows
the level of your skill in judo.
Judo experts who take part in
the Olympic Games must have a black belt.

Karate is another popular sport.
Speed and agility are very important
for karate students.

Students at a karate school learn how
to defend themselves from attack.

In a karate match, the attacker
uses fists, feet, knees, fingers,
and the edge of the hand to strike
the other person's body.

In karate, each person tries to
put all their skill and power into
where they hit their opponent.

A karate expert can break
bricks or planks of wood with
one blow of the hand or foot.

Index

Editorial Consultant: Donna Bailey
Executive Editor: Elizabeth Strauss
Project Editor: Becky Ward

Picture research by Jennifer Garratt
Designed by Richard Garratt Design

Photographs
All photographs by Peter Greenland except:
Cover: Hutchison Library
All Sport: 28 (Tony Duffy)
Hutchison Library: 26, 29
Sporting Pictures: 27, 30, 31, 32

Library of Congress Cataloging-in-Publication Data: Bailey, Donna. Judo / Donna Bailey. p. cm.—(Sports world) Includes index. Summary: Beginning judo students learn the skills, techniques, and exercises that help them master this art of unarmed self-defense. ISBN 0-8114-2900-8 1. Judo—Juvenile literature. [1. Judo.] I. Title. II. Series: Bailey, Donna. Sports world. GV1114.B35 1991 796.8′152—dc20 90-23058 CIP AC

ISBN 0-8114-2900-8
Copyright 1991 Steck-Vaughn Company
Original copyright Heinemann Children's Reference 1991
All rights reserved. No part of the material protected by this copyright may be reproduced or utilized in any form or by any means, electronic or mechanical, including photocopying, recording, or by any information storage and retrieval system, without permission in writing from the copyright owner. Requests for permission to make copies of any part of the work should be mailed to: Copyright Permissions, Steck-Vaughn Company, P.O. Box 26015, Austin, Texas 78755. Printed in the United States of America.

1 2 3 4 5 6 7 8 9 0 LB 96 95 94 93 92 91

Norwood Grade School Library
Dist. R 2 Jt.